T0055931

Piano Time Dance

Pauline Hall

MUSIC DEPARTMENT

OXFORD
UNIVERSITY PRESS

OXFORD
UNIVERSITY PRESS

Great Clarendon Street, Oxford OX2 6DP, England

Oxford University Press is a department of the University of Oxford.
It furthers the University's aim of excellence in research, scholarship,
and education by publishing worldwide

Oxford is a registered trade mark of Oxford University Press
in the UK and in certain other countries

This collection © Oxford University Press 2012

Each composer has asserted his/her right under the Copyright, Designs
and Patents Act, 1988, to be identified as the Composer of their Work(s).

Pauline Hall has asserted her right under the Copyright, Designs
and Patents Act, 1988, to be identified as the Editor of this Work.

Database right Oxford University Press (maker)

First published 2012
Photocopying or arranging this copyright material is ILLEGAL

All rights reserved. No part of this publication may be reproduced,
stored in a retrieval system, or transmitted, in any form or by any means,
without the prior permission in writing of Oxford University Press

Permission to perform the works in this anthology in public
(except in the course of divine worship) should normally be obtained
from a local performing right licensing organization, unless the owner
or the occupier of the premises being used already holds a licence from
such an organization. Likewise, permission to make and exploit a recording
of these works should be obtained from a local mechanical copyright
licensing organization

Enquiries concerning reproduction outside the scope of the above should be
directed to the Music Rights Department, Oxford University Press,
at music.permissions.uk@oup.com or at the address above

9 10

ISBN 978–0–19–337005–0

Illustrations by Andy Hammond
Music and text origination by
Katie Johnston
Printed in Great Britain on acid-free paper by
Halstan & Co. Ltd., Amersham, Bucks.

With thanks to Jan Bullard for advising on piece selection and fingering.

Contents

Hoofer's Delight	5
Allemande	6
Needles and Pins	7
Chatterbox Charlie	8
Forget-me-not Waltz	9
Hornpipe	10
Gigue à l'Angloise	11
Ch-ch-chilly Cha-cha-cha	12
Gavotte from Trio Sonata in D, Op. 5 No. 2 HWV 397	13
Perfect Polka	14
'Clog Dance' from the ballet *La fille mal gardée*	15
Latin Moves	16
Sarabande from Keyboard Suite No. 4 in D minor HWV 437	17
Festival Mazurka	18
Minuet from Keyboard Sonata No. 5 in G Hob. XVI:11	19
Tango Misterio	20
Blue Train	21
The Soft-shoe Shuffle	22
The Trot of Mr Fox	23
Circle Dance	24
Disco Baroque	25
Aces High	26
Two-tone Tango	28
Amber's Samba	30

Hoofer's Delight

A 'hoofer' is a tap dancer. Many of the early hoofers started their careers by dancing on street corners, in cities across America.

Philip Croydon

Earthy, with swing

© Oxford University Press 2012. Photocopying this copyright material is ILLEGAL.

Allemande

The allemande was an elegant dance that probably came from Germany. It was popular during the late seventeenth century.

© Oxford University Press 2012. Photocopying this copyright material is ILLEGAL.

Needles and Pins

This is an example of a Morris dance, a cheerful English folk dance that is performed by groups of dancers carrying sticks and wearing costumes decorated with flowers and bells.

Melody anon.
arr. Alan Bullard

Lively, with bounce

mf

Fine

f

D.C. al Fine

p

mf

© Oxford University Press 2012. Photocopying this copyright material is ILLEGAL.

Chatterbox Charlie

This dance is a calypso, a style that comes from the West Indies. The calypso is often used in Caribbean Carnivals, and the music includes steel drums.

Paul Drayton

© Oxford University Press 2012. Photocopying this copyright material is ILLEGAL.

Forget-me-not Waltz

A waltz is a ballroom dance that was fashionable in Vienna two hundred years ago and is still popular today.

Stephen Duro

© Oxford University Press 2012. Photocopying this copyright material is ILLEGAL.

Hornpipe

The hornpipe was danced by sailors in the days of the old sailing ships.

Pauline Hall

Bright and breezy

mf

LH

mp

cresc.

f

© Oxford University Press 2012. Photocopying this copyright material is ILLEGAL.

Gigue à l'Angloise

The French gigue is a lively and energetic dance that is sometimes known as a jig. The title of this piece means 'gigue in the English style'.

Georg Philipp Telemann (1681–1767)
arr. Pauline Hall

© Oxford University Press 2012. Photocopying this copyright material is ILLEGAL.

Ch-ch-chilly Cha-cha-cha

The cha-cha-cha is a 1950s ballroom dance that takes its name from its distinctive rhythm. Here, the staccatos give the music a chilly and shivery feel.

Very crisp and shivery

Paul Drayton

© Oxford University Press 2012. Photocopying this copyright material is ILLEGAL.

Gavotte from Trio Sonata in D, Op. 5 No. 2 HWV 397

Originally a lively French folk dance, the gavotte later became an elegant dance that was popular at the French royal court.

George Frideric Handel (1685–1759)
ed. Maisie Aldridge

Allegro

f

p

cresc.

f

© Oxford University Press 1969 and 2012. Photocopying this copyright material is ILLEGAL.

© Oxford University Press 2012. Photocopying this copyright material is ILLEGAL.

'Clog Dance' from the ballet La fille mal gardée

Imagine having to dance to this music wearing wooden clogs! For the tapping bars, tap with your knuckles on the piano lid.

Peter Ludwig Hertel (1817–99)
arr. Pauline Hall

Heavily

mf

f

tap

1.

2.

© Oxford University Press 2012. Photocopying this copyright material is ILLEGAL.

Latin Moves

This is an example of a rumba, a Latin American dance originally from Cuba. It is usually accompanied by percussion instruments such as claves and maracas.

Alan Haughton

© Oxford University Press 2012. Photocopying this copyright material is ILLEGAL.

Sarabande from Keyboard Suite No. 4 in D minor HWV 437

The sarabande is a slow, stately dance in three time. Notice that this sarabande is in 3/2 time, which means that you count three minims in each bar.

George Frideric Handel (1685–1759)
arr. Pauline Hall

Slow and solemn

mf

rit.

© Oxford University Press 2012. Photocopying this copyright material is ILLEGAL.

Festival Mazurka

The mazurka is a dance from Poland with accented rhythms that mimic the movements of the dancers.

Alan Bullard

© Oxford University Press 2012. Photocopying this copyright material is ILLEGAL.

© Oxford University Press 2012. Photocopying this copyright material is ILLEGAL.

© Oxford University Press 2012. Photocopying this copyright material is ILLEGAL.

Blue Train

This swing dance is in the blues style and should feel very relaxed and laid-back.

David Cullen

Moderato

mf

rall.

© Oxford University Press 2012. Photocopying this copyright material is ILLEGAL.

The Soft-shoe Shuffle

The soft-shoe shuffle is danced using steps from the tap dance. Instead of wearing metal-soled tap shoes, the dancer wears shoes with soft soles.

Nikki Iles

© Oxford University Press 2012. Photocopying this copyright material is ILLEGAL.

The Trot of Mr Fox

The foxtrot is a gliding ballroom dance that was one of the most popular dances of the 1920s and 1930s.

David Cullen

© Oxford University Press 2012. Photocopying this copyright material is ILLEGAL.

Circle Dance

This piece is in the style of an eastern European folk dance often performed at weddings. The bride sits on a raised chair while the guests dance around her in a circle, with the music getting faster and faster.

Nikki Iles

Steady

mf

f

p

mf

Faster

f

© Oxford University Press 2012. Photocopying this copyright material is ILLEGAL.

Disco Baroque

Disco dominated popular music during the late 1970s. Using similar sequences to those found in earlier music, this piece suggests the rhythmic disco feel with a steady drum beat, which should be maintained (in your head!) in the middle section.

© Oxford University Press 2012. Photocopying this copyright material is ILLEGAL.

Aces High

Anthony Marks

© Oxford University Press 2012. Photocopying this copyright material is ILLEGAL.

Aces High

This is an example of reggae, a popular music style that originated in Jamaica and has strong off-beats.

Anthony Marks

© Oxford University Press 2012. Photocopying this copyright material is ILLEGAL.

Two-tone Tango

Paul Drayton

© Oxford University Press 2012. Photocopying this copyright material is ILLEGAL.

Two-tone Tango

This is another Latin American tango.

Paul Drayton

© Oxford University Press 2012. Photocopying this copyright material is ILLEGAL.

Amber's Samba

David Cullen

© Oxford University Press 2012. Photocopying this copyright material is ILLEGAL.

Amber's Samba

The samba is a lively dance from Brazil that often features in Carnival parades.

David Cullen

© Oxford University Press 2012. Photocopying this copyright material is ILLEGAL.